She
Loves Me
She Loves
Me Not

Contents

She Loves Me Not ...
Friendship Don'ts

She Loves
Me Not ...

Friendship Dont's

CHAPTER ONE

Don't discourage her dreams —

nobody likes a wet blanket!

*****

But every road is tough to me
that has no friend to cheer it.

ELIZABETH SHANE

Recently I was on a talk show that included a panel of women who I had never met before. We had a great time on the show talking about different subjects, and answering letters from viewers. It was an energetic program that required quick thinking and an ability to express thoughts clearly. After the show, I complimented one of the women on her genuine style and her gentle heart. I then made the comment that if we lived in the same city we could probably be friends. It was just a simple statement made with a smile, but I could tell she was totally taken aback as she said, 'What a nice thing to say, thank you'. It wasn't hard for me to do, and my few encouraging words were a blessing to her.

Our words are powerful tools that can bring hurt or healing. Let's be determined to be the friend whose words bring life. Words are like gifts we give each other. I remember one Christmas getting a letter from a friend who lived in my city. She said that money was a little scarce for her right now, but she wanted to give me a present. What she gave me is just as valuable as a store-bought gift, maybe more so. She gave me the gift of words. She wrote a letter of encouragement to me, telling me which of my qualities had been a blessing to her over the years (she focused on the good ones ... there are some!), and what she hoped for me in the future. This letter meant so much to me that I still have it! Actually I have kept quite a few of the encouraging notes I have received over the years, and on days when I am having a tough time, I pull them out and have a read! Enjoy this story from *Chicken Soup for the Soul* by Jack Canfield and Mark Victor Hansen:

In the first grade, Mr Lohr said my purple tepee wasn't realistic enough, that purple was no colour for a tent, that purple was a colour for people who died, that my drawing wasn't good enough to hang with the others. I walked back to my seat counting the swish swish swishes of my baggy corduroy trousers. With a black crayon, nightfall came to my purple tent in the middle of an afternoon.

In second grade, Mr Barta said, 'Draw anything.' He didn't care what. I left my paper blank and when he came around to my desk, my heart beat like a tom-tom while he touched my head with his big hand and in a soft voice said, 'The snowfall. How clean and white and beautiful'.[1]

See the good in what your friend is doing. Be the encourager. Don't be the friend who is a master at life-liposuction — sucking all the life out of someone. You be the one putting life into situations!

Watch out for being critical and impatient, expecting your friend to always make the right decision. We don't always get it right either, so let's dish out the encouragement we ourselves need. We are all going to fail from time to time. We are all going to make mistakes. What most of us want when we make a mistake is someone to help us up, fix what needs fixing, and encourage us on the journey once again. Those of us who find fault, as if it were buried treasure, need to change how we see things. It is easy to point out the mistakes someone else is making. The challenge, for those of us willing to take it, is to find the good in someone and give the gift of encouragement today to those you come in contact with. You'd be amazed at the ripple effect that can have. It is a gift that can change lives.

When you offer encouragement to someone, it keeps you from being self-centred ... which we all can be! I have come to realize that the success of my life is in my ability to be an encouragement and a help to others. The more I encourage others, the more successful my life will be.

Most of us are surrounded all day by negativity from within and without. Some of us question whether we can do whatever it is we started to do. If we are in a tough situation ... a relationship, family or job crisis ... then an encouraging word can be the difference between giving up on the situation or hanging in there. Sometimes we are entering a new arena, facing a new, perhaps exciting, challenge and still we might wonder if we can really do it. Encouraging words from a friend can make all the difference in the world. Last year I was on a plane from Sydney to Los Angeles and found myself flying with two of my favourite girlfriends on the planet ... lucky me! This trip was just after my first book, *dumb things we do*, was published and I really hadn't taken the time to celebrate (and I do like any excuse for a celebration!). Before the plane had even taken off, we grabbed a glass and made a toast. The really great thing was that we each congratulated each other on recent accomplishments. What we said wasn't shallow. We took the time to say something meaningful ... right there in the bulkhead seat! Shanelle, an officer with the United Nations; Chris, a public speaker who has changed the lives of thousands of young people with her inspirational talks, and I are each doing different things fulfilling our purpose on the earth. And we are truly excited about each other's feats. We just grabbed a few moments out of eternity to encourage each other. As I looked in their faces, I felt loved and supported in a way that motivates me to succeed. I felt as if I could conquer my part of the world. What a gift they gave me. You can do the same ... encourage and celebrate with the women in your life. The gift you give will be priceless.

The word encourage means 'to put courage in', and courage means 'facing danger in spite of fear'. As we encourage our friends we are saying, 'Keep going! You can do it!' Recently I was embarking on a new challenge in an area I'd never done anything in before, and I was a little nervous. My friend Laura, who had just moved into a new house with three young sons and a thousand boxes to unpack, somehow found the time to write me a note telling me that she believed in me and was confident that I would do well. And my friend LeeAnn sent me a very colourful e-mail that said, 'YOU CAN DO IT!!' (She's a sanguine, and sanguines use colours, exclamation marks and capitals a lot!) I began my new adventure ready to succeed. How thankful I am for my encouraging friends.

FRIENDSHIP POWER POINTS

here's what to do . . .

- say two encouraging things to your friends today

- say an encouraging, complimentary word to someone you don't even know

- if your friend is starting to doubt her dream, you be the one to tell her to keep going for it.

Chapter Two

Not liking who you are —

what's not to like?

*Friendship with oneself is all-important because
without it one cannot be friends with anyone else
in the world.*

ELEANOR ROOSEVELT

I have seen more friendships totally messed up because one
of the friends isn't confident about who she is. She is
wrestling with feelings of insecurity. However, to truly be a
friend to someone else, we must like ourselves. We must
like who we are created to be. I'm not talking about self-
centred self-love, but the quiet confidence that we get from

knowing that we were put on the planet to fulfil a purpose, and that everything required to fulfil our mission is available to us.

Here's how you can tell if you don't like yourself. Can you freely give compliments or encouragement? Are you excited when a friend accomplishes something important in her life? Or are you envious? What if it is something that you would like to accomplish as well? Be honest. In Chapter Four of *She loves me* ... I mentioned that not remaining loyal when something great happens to your friend or when she reaches a goal is a sign of jealousy. Jealousy is a sign of our own insecurity. Why is it that we couldn't give a compliment? Perhaps because deep down we feel it would take away from us ... or it would give our friend a big head. The size of her ego is not your responsibility. Your job is to freely encourage, freely give compliments. I compliment people regularly, because I know who I am and I like myself. Giving compliments in no way depletes who I am. I will not be emptied if I give out a hundred compliments a day. In a healthy friendship, we desire to see our friend reach her potential, building her up and encouraging her along the way. Check your own heart. When was the last time you complimented someone without expecting anything back? If you can't remember, then perhaps you need to work on how you see yourself.

When you walk into a room, either at a party or a business meeting, what do you feel? What are you thinking? Are you wondering if anyone there will like you? Are you trying to figure out what you can do so they will? Are you wondering if you will have to change to be friends with them? We should walk into a room as whole, healthy women, knowing that there will be people who like us and, if not, then there will be a next time. I'm not talking about the arrogant 'take me or leave me' attitude, because we certainly all need to be humble realizing that we should grow and learn things from others. There are changes that we all must make if we want to live a fulfilling life. We make these changes not so others will like us (although, if they do, that's a nice by-product!), but so that *we* like us and are equipped to fulfil our purpose.

Another way to realize that you don't really like yourself is if you find you can't make a decision. Now, I am aware there are some personality types — the choleric and the sanguine — that are quick to make decisions (and not all of them the right ones!), but all of us should be able to do this. If you find yourself continually wavering, unable to confidently make a decision, then I would like to suggest that perhaps the reason is a low self-confidence. I believe that not liking yourself is the root of low self-confidence. Perhaps as a child, you weren't encouraged, praised or motivated to succeed by loving parents or carers. Thus, it makes sense that you would have very little confidence in who you are. Now, as a grown-up, it's time to rebuild the confidence and learn to like yourself. It is possible! Leave the past where it belongs ... in the past!

Not liking yourself is one of the most serious toxins in any friendship, and is often at the root of other problems. Some people are overly dependent on other people, and instead need to discover their own strength. As women, our tendency towards total dependency on our friends can be a serious weakness. It's important to love our friends and be committed to them, but we shouldn't be totally dependent on them for our strength, bleeding the life out of them. Friends add to our life; they shouldn't be our life. We can't look to our friends to fill us up.

Judith Viorst, in her book *Necessary Losses*, tells us that we have to have a self in order to be a friend. To have a self means we have an 'inner core'.

As Brenda Hunter writes in *In the Company of Women*:

> We like ourselves for the most part, and we can be
> alone and enjoy our own company. We don't use our
> friends as a way of escaping our feelings of boredom,
> emptiness or even self-hatred. We need to be
> comfortable inside our own skin to be comfortable in
> friendships. We need to develop our own interests,
> hobbies and goals that we occasionally pursue alone.
> We need to balance time spent with our friends with
> time spent in solitude.[2]

A friend is to walk with you on your journey; she can't take your journey for you.

When you like who you are, you are more fun to be around. Recently I was on a stage speaking to hundreds of women, and I thought I was looking pretty cute! I was having a good hair day; I liked the outfit I was wearing ... a long black skirt, a little black t-shirt with a very colourful halter over it. I'm sure I was in the middle of making a life-changing point when all of a sudden my halter just fell off! Right when you think you have it all together, something like this happens! If I hadn't had that little black t-shirt on under the halter, those women would have seen something

14

they hadn't paid for! Was I embarrassed? A little. Did I cry? No. Was I angry? No. Did I leave the stage? No. Have I since learned to tie my halters very tightly? YES! Sometimes things like this happen to us and, instead of laughing, we let the circumstance rob us of our confidence.

In the 1980s I was working as an actress in Los Angeles. One of my first jobs in television was a lead character in a night-time soap opera. (You know, one of those really educational shows!) I was supposed to be the pretty, young female heart-throb in the show ... which basically means I was in a bikini or lingerie the entire time! I was a bit nervous because this was my first really big part. As I was being fitted for my wardrobe and the different skimpy outfits I would be wearing, the producers decided that my figure was not curvy enough. To remedy this situation, they placed a mastectomy pad in my bikini top. The first scene I was to film involved a conflict between my stepfather and me. We were at the beach and after our fight I was to get away from him by running down the beach with my dog. I took off running, cameras were rolling and one of the mastectomy pads flew out of my bikini top and hit the sand. I stopped. The dog stopped. I looked at the pad in the sand. The dog looked at the pad in the sand. I knew at that moment that I could have laughed, cried or been mad at the wardrobe people for not sewing the pad into the bikini top. I chose to laugh. The director yelled, 'Cut!' Wardrobe people came over to remedy the situation ... which involved a needle and thread! Was I embarrassed? Yes. But because I knew that I was more than my job, I could see the funny side of it. Acting was never my life, only a job. If we would see our lives as more than any single part of it, it would be easier to laugh at the mistakes that undoubtedly will come along.

Once my friend Shanelle, the United Nations officer, was flying from one country to another, seated next to someone she needed to impress. She was speaking very eloquently, and I'm sure was saying brilliant things, when the flight attendant came by offering Popsicles. Shanelle took one and stuck it in her mouth, not realizing that it had, until recently, been in dry ice. The Popsicle quickly stuck to her lips as she wrapped them around it. She could do nothing! The man she was trying to impress watched as she turned to him with a Popsicle stuck to her mouth. She flagged down the flight attendant and gestured that she was stuck. The flight attendant brought a warm cloth and she put it to her mouth and the Popsicle was finally released. It took her a minute to get up the nerve to look the very important man in the face, but eventually she did. She still meets with dignitaries and presidents all over the world. She manages to laugh at herself, knowing that, in spite of all the funny, weird stuff that happens, she will accomplish her purpose. Don't take yourself quite so seriously … laugh when you do something silly or when something funny happens. Confident women can … and that is your goal … to be that confident woman!

When you like who you are you don't spend time wanting what someone else has, or get frustrated and jealous that you don't have their abilities. I heard this true story about a man in South Africa who sold his land to go looking for diamonds. He knew they had been found in his country and he wanted to find his share. He travelled all over the country and ended up losing his family and his home in his quest to find diamonds … and he found nothing. Meanwhile, the man who had bought *his* land found the largest diamond ever and the land became the largest diamond-producing area. So many of us are looking for, and wanting the talents and the purpose that others have … we spend valuable time wishing we were like someone else and all the time we have our own treasure inside us … just waiting to be discovered.

It is hard to love our friend if we don't love who we were created to be. We just can't like anyone else if we don't like ourselves. I know there are some of you who aren't confident in yourself — you don't really like who you are. Now, I am not talking about the fact that some of us might not like something about our bodies. (I haven't met a woman yet who wouldn't change at least one thing on her body! There is not a house I have lived in that I haven't made improvements or changes to and I am going to be living in my body for ninety plus years … so I'm sure I'll make a few improvements!) But I would not be making the changes to give me a sense of purpose or to cause me to like myself any better. There are women who make all the outside changes and are still lost and confused. So, make the changes if you want, just realize that they are not going to fix your heart. But there are some things you can do if you want to build your confidence … if you want to learn to love who you are.

FRIENDSHIP POWER POINTS

here's what to do . . .

- tell yourself out loud that you are worth liking

- laugh at some of the silly things you have done

- realize that your friendships depend on you liking you!

Chapter Three

Not knowing who you are —

who are you anyway?

Until you make peace with who you are, you'll never be content with what you have.

Doris Mortman

You were put on the planet on purpose! You are not some accident … no matter what your parents told you. There is something specific you were created to do. When we discover our life mission then we feel a sense of purpose, and begin to feel confident in who we are. So many children (perhaps you too) have been taught they are basically just exploded tadpoles, randomly on the earth with no particular purpose in mind. With this kind of teaching out there, it is no wonder a lot of us feel no sense of purpose and don't truly value the life we have been given. And when you don't value your life, then you mess it up, either with drugs, bad relationships or a myriad of other things. YOUR LIFE HAS VALUE! THERE IS A REASON YOU ARE ON THE PLANET! I need you to get this . . . can you tell?

In around 1200 AD, women were told that we were simply chattel — property. Basically we were told that we were one step above an oxen or cow in the order of things. Then in the 1970s women were told that if we wanted to fulfil our purpose, we had to act, dress and think like a man. And today I see a resurgence of some ancient myths that women are goddesses. I would like to suggest that we are not a cow, a man or a goddess! We are woman. Why do we feel the need to embellish that? We shouldn't. Being a woman is wonderful. As women there is so much we were put on the earth to accomplish. Let's discover it!

I know that my destiny — the reason I was put on the planet — will involve other people. None of us is supposed to be the Lone Ranger. Together we can accomplish great things, but only if each of us likes who we are, knows our purpose and is confidently committed to fulfilling it.

I'm NOT talking about self-centred, self-serving and self-indulgent confidence, or the confidence that comes from anger, but rather the confidence that comes from a sense of security — a confidence that allows you to help someone else and to give to someone else. A woman who truly knows herself can give freely, knowing that it doesn't take anything away from her, because she has plenty on the inside.

Be honest with yourself. Do you see signs that perhaps you don't know or like who you are created to be? Well, begin the process today! Know that you have a purpose of fulfil on the planet. As Cynthia Kersey, in her book *Unstoppable*, says, purpose can:

> ignite your spirit, providing personal meaning and deep satisfaction to your life. Purpose is the why — why you are here — and your own special calling. Purpose is the unique gifts and insights that you bring to the planet and can contribute to your world. Purpose fuels your efforts and gives you the drive to continue, no matter what the challenges.[3]

Mel Gibson portraying William Wallace in the movie *Braveheart* said, 'Every man dies, but not every man really lives'. Most people aren't really living their lives with passion and a sense of purpose, but instead are just enduring, waiting, wondering and hoping something good happens to them. We can't be like that! We should be living our lives with vitality, an excitement and a true joy that we are accomplishing what we are on the planet to accomplish.

So how do you discover your purpose? There are great books out there written just to help us figure it out, and there are many seminars offered to encourage us in finding our purpose. So read one or two books, and go to a few seminars. But I'll give a few quick pointers here. Discovering your purpose is a process. Ask yourself how you want to be remembered ... by your husband and children ... by your co-workers ... by your world. Are the things you are doing now helping achieve that goal? If not, change what you are doing.

If you want to be remembered by your children as a mother who was encouraging, loving and inspiring, are you being that now? If you want your community to see you as caring for those who are less fortunate than you, are you doing that now? List some words that describe you now. List what jobs you are doing now. Then list some causes that excite you. These are all things that can help you understand your purpose each day. Now you can set goals that will help you accomplish your purpose. A lot of people set goals and then get frustrated because they don't achieve them ... that's because these goals have very little to do with their purpose, so there is no excitement or motivation.

Here's the process. Perhaps you want to be remembered by your community as someone who helped the underdog, as someone who cared for people. And maybe you describe yourself as compassionate, tender-hearted, and a lover of people. Right now you are teaching at a kindergarten and the cause that stirs you is finding a way to make life easier and more fun for disabled children. You love to help with Special Olympics and other events like that. Your purpose on the planet will in some way be related to compassionately teaching and helping children who are developmentally disabled. So taking a basket-weaving class may be fun for a moment, but you may not finish it because it doesn't relate to your purpose ... unless you are going to weave baskets for the kids! Set goals that relate to your passion ... your purpose.

And as you are pursuing that purpose, and reaching a goal, you will probably encounter obstacles. (Just thought I'd warn you ... if you haven't encountered any yet!) When you overcome the obstacles you run into, amazing things happen inside you. Let's say that in order to fulfil your destiny you need to lose 45 kilos. You begin a diet program and begin to exercise because now you see that whether or not you fulfil your destiny can affect all of us. Losing 45 kilos is not easy to say the least. Many obstacles will come up to try to defeat you. Haagen Daz's icecream still looks good. The gym you joined will move your work-out class to 6 am instead of the reasonable 8 am. Your boyfriend breaks up with you, so of course you deserve to eat until you feel better. All of these are obstacles that can sidetrack you from fulfilling your vision. When you don't allow them to knock you off course and you reach your goal, something happens inside you. You feel amazing. You set a goal and reached it. A lot of people start things, but you actually finished something!

Someone recently asked me if they should like who they were created to be or who they have become. Actually it is a little of both. I believe I have been put on the earth to fulfil a mission, and I have been given certain gifts in order to accomplish it. That's the created part. I need to discover my mission, like it, fully embrace it, at the same time enjoying the gifts in others ... not wasting time coveting them. I enjoy watching amazing women athletes, realizing they are using the gifts given to them. I also love listening to singers who make music come alive. I am neither a singer nor an athlete. I have discovered the gifts given to me and I am in the process of figuring out how to grow them. The gifts given to us to fulfil our mission are only in seed form. It then becomes our responsibility to grow them to maturity and thus become the woman we were destined to be.

Knowing you were created with a purpose and then overcoming the obstacles on the way to fulfilling that purpose, creates a strength inside you that develops no other way. And when that strength is there it allows you to be a better friend — one who is free to give and free to love.

FRIENDSHIP POWER POINTS

here's what to do . . .

- know that you are one-of-a-kind, irreplaceable and wonderful

- begin the process of discovering your purpose on the planet — YOU DO HAVE ONE!

CHAPTER FOUR

Not fighting fair —

yes ... there are rules!

*****

*... the responsibilities of friendship? ... To talk.
And to listen.*

ROSIE THOMAS

You love her ... you want to smack her ... you love
her ... you want to yell at her ... you love her ... you
can't believe she just said that ... you love her ... oh ... she
makes you so mad! What's a girl to do?

Conflicts will arise between good friends. What do you
do when your friend hurts your feelings? What do you
do when you see something in your friend that can ultimately

27

destroy the friendship? Can you agree to disagree or do you let the disagreement cause you to pull away?

Some of us may have been raised in homes where any conflict was abusive, where all disagreements got out of hand. But it doesn't have to be like this. And the truth is ... I never know what kind of friendship I have until we manage to survive a rough patch. Then I know I have a friend who is willing to work with me to create a great relationship. Brant R. Burleson, professor of communication at Purdue University in Indiana, says, 'The better friends you are, the more likely you'll face conflicts'. So, yes, disagreements will arise, and there are ways to handle them so the friendship stays intact.

The first way to handle the disagreement is to actually *handle* it! Don't pretend it did not happen. Don't pull away and give up on the friendship. (I am not talking about if your friend had an affair with your husband — in this case she is not your friend ... and your core values are too different for a friendship to ever work. I'm talking about the little things we let add up until we explode — she is late to meet you for the 100th time ... she forgot to return the skirt she borrowed ...). Pulling away won't mend the friendship and it won't help your heart either. We need to be willing to friendship dont's

confront the issue that is seemingly dividing us — however big or small. Many people are afraid of confrontation because they see it as a bad thing. Confrontation means coming 'face to face'. It is bringing an issue to the light so a relationship might be restored instead of destroyed. Confrontation is not attacking, abusive or the voicing of petty and nasty criticism. Confrontation is bringing an issue to light so that the friendship is restored and strengthened.

Sometimes you need to swallow your pride in order to mend the friendship. Denise had to when a friendship turned sour. Her story is told by Patricia Skalka in her article 'How to Mend a Friendship', in *Reader's Digest*, June 1999:

> For nearly four months, Denise had watched over her friend Nora's two younger daughters who were living with their father on a military base in Hawaii, while Nora completed training as a dental hygienist in a different state. Denise said that she felt honoured to be asked to step in. When Nora returned at Christmas, Denise was excited because she had so much to tell her. But Nora never called. One of the girls even had a birthday party that Denise was not invited to. Denise said that she felt used. At first,

Denise vowed to avoid Nora. Then she decided to swallow her pride and let her friend know how she felt. Nora admitted that she had been so worried about being separated from her family that she'd been blind to what Denise had done to help her. Today she admits that she never would have figured out what happened if Denise hadn't called her on it. When a friend hurts you, your instinct is to protect yourself, but that makes it harder to patch up problems.[4]

Once my friend Wendy said that she had something she needed to talk to me about. She then proceeded to tell me in a rather sheepish manner that she 'hated my perfume'. Now you might be thinking, 'Why would she tell you something that really doesn't matter?' Well, we were about to take a fourteen-hour plane trip together, sitting side by side, and the fragrance I wore bothered her. There are a few responses to a comment like that. One is to say, 'Too bad for you. This is my favourite perfume and I am wearing it. You'll just have to sit at the other end of the plane from me'. The other is to say, 'No problem. I won't wear this one while I am around you'. This may seem like a silly example, but I have seen friendships destroyed because of examples just as silly! I truly appreciate the fact that Wendy was willing to tell me what the problem was instead of just booking a seat at the other end of the plane and leaving me wondering what was going on, maybe with hurt feelings. And I am a big enough girl to not get offended because she doesn't like my perfume. I did not take it personally. The friendship is more valuable to me than my perfume.

Sometimes conflict arises because we each have unspoken rules we expect everyone to obey. Perhaps while you were growing up your mother never really let you help in the kitchen because it was her domain. Now you are at university and you go to a friend's house for dinner. After dinner you continue to sit at the table talking to your friend who is in the kitchen cleaning up. It never occurs to you to offer to help, because you were raised thinking that the kitchen belongs to the woman of the house. On the other hand, your friend is getting angrier the longer you continue to sit there because she was raised with the rule that everyone helps in the kitchen. If neither of you says anything, I guarantee you will never be invited to dinner again and you will never really know why. (By the way, when you come to my house, feel free to wash the dishes!)

I have a friend who has this rule that work-related questions can only be asked at work — not when we are out playing. She got angry with me the first time I asked a work question but I didn't know her rule, and she assumed everyone did. This is also true in a marriage. Most of the time we enter a marriage with unspoken rules, or notions of how we think marriage should be. I remember thinking that every man should know how to run a barbecue. Well, my husband didn't even know what charcoal was! And I thought the man was supposed to be able to fix anything that needed fixing … silly me! If it requires more than a hammer, my husband can't fix it. Of course, he thought all women could iron. Boy, was he in for a shock! So, if there are things that are important to you, make sure you are communicating them and not just assuming everyone knows.

In a conflict, it helps to be able to see the situation from the other person's point of view. This is not easy because most of us selfishly think our side of the story is the true one! (Okay maybe you're not like that, but I know I can be!) Sociologist Rebecca Adams of the University of North Carolina and Rosemary Blieszner, professor of gerontology and family studies at the Virginia Polytechnic Institute and State University, interviewed fifty-three adults each of whom had many friendships lasting decades. 'We were curious how these people managed to sustain strong friendships for so long,' says Rosemary. Tolerance is the key, the researchers learned. The subjects also didn't let problems get blown out of proportion. It's surprising how often a dispute results from a simple misunderstanding.

Jan Yager, author of *Friendshifts: The Power of Friendship and How It Shapes Our Lives,* recalls what happened after her father died and a close friend didn't attend the funeral. 'I felt hurt and disappointed,' she says. Later Jan learned that her friend hadn't come to the service because she was still distraught over her own father's death. 'My perspective changed entirely,' says Jan. 'Rather than feeling slighted, I empathized with my friend.' Instead of immediately assuming the worst about our friend, perhaps we should give her a chance to explain.

Rick Warren, a great leader, said he's noticed that there are a few different ways people respond to conflict. The first is ... 'my way'. This response is the 'I fight until I win' response. 'I have to be the winner. You are totally wrong and I will fight you until you give up!'

The next response to conflict is ... 'no way'. The person who responds this way always gives in to conflict. They avoid it. There is no way you are getting them into a fight. They withdraw, pull back and ignore the problem. This may keep the friendship calm but nothing is ever resolved.

Another response to conflict is … 'your way'. The person that responds this way always gives in. They are the doormat. They want approval so badly that they roll over and play dead. Again, this may keep the relationship calm, but it also produces a lot of bitterness.

'Half-way' is another response. 'You give in half the time and I give in half the time.' This is certainly a better response than previous ones, but there is a better way to communicate.

'Our way' is the best way to handle conflict. This is when we work out mutual goals together. We do what's best for the friendship — not just for one of us. We care about the friendship more than any issue.

For any issue to be resolved, we need a sit-down-and-face-the-issues conference. And usually more than one. Conflict is rarely solved accidentally. It must be deliberate and intentional. Conflict is rarely solved on the run. Be prepared to fix the problem — not cast blame. Come ready to reconcile and resolve.

There are certain ground rules that have to be observed in conflict resolution. During the Cold War, the United

States and Russia had treaties to ban certain weapons in the event of conflict. This was not because both countries were in total agreement on certain issues, they just realized that nuclear weapons could destroy them both. Perhaps it is the same in a friendship. We must eliminate verbal weapons that will do more harm than good. Watch for using words like 'always' and 'never', because usually they aren't true. And then, of course, remember what you tell your children: no hitting, no biting, no lying, no throwing things, no bad words!

If you have had a conflict in a friendship, be willing to apologize ... even if you were the one wronged. The movie *Love Story* made the comment that 'love is never having to say you're sorry'. But I believe love is about being the first one to say, 'I'm sorry'. And then maybe the one who made the mistake can explain or admit her failure.

Hopefully I have given you some tools in helping you negotiate the conflicts that come in friendship. Although there will be some people that we might need to let go of, there will be more we should hang on to. So don't give up on the relationship just because of a minor conflict that has escalated into a big issue. Do your best to resolve it ... even if it takes more than one attempt. As long as you are talking to one another, there is hope for resolution. Work hard to maintain the connection, as friendships naturally go through ups and downs. Don't abandon the treasure you have in your friendship.

FRIENDSHIP POWER POINTS

here's what to do . . .

- don't let an unresolved issue separate you from your friend
- try to see the issue from her point of view
- set a time to have a resolve-the-issue talk
- if it doesn't work the first time, try again.

CHAPTER FIVE

Don't betray that friend —

ouch, that hurts!

* * * * *

Friendship is a strong and habitual inclination in two persons to promote the good and happiness of one another.

EUSTACE BUDGELL

I don't know of anything that hurts more than hearing a secret you told a friend on the lips of someone else. Realizing that the friend you thought you could trust with the issues of your heart has betrayed you is painful ... and yet we have probably all been the betrayer as well as the one betrayed at some point in our life.

Gossip is a form of betrayal and should be seen as such. It is not just afternoon entertainment. Betrayal is involved because you are sharing a secret that should have remained in your own heart. Generally, as women, we are more willing to make ourselves vulnerable to one another and so we have more 'dirt to spill'. (This is why women generally have more friends than men, because real friendships are based on intimacy, not just shared activities.) Our vulnerability is good for intimacy, but we often aren't trustworthy with the same sharing of thoughts and feelings that bring us closer together. Why is it that we are tempted to be faithless? Perhaps it is because we need to prove to someone else that we are on the 'inside circle'. When we share something that was confided to us, we are basically saying to someone else, 'I know something you don't know'. In some way or another, it makes us feel important. I would like to suggest that we KNOCK IT OFF! When you like who you are, you don't feel the need to prove anything to anyone.

If someone shares a dream, a fear, a thought or a hope with you, be grateful that you have a friend who is willing to be intimate with you, and keep the revelation to yourself. Sometimes someone might share something with you that you don't feel right in keeping to yourself ... suicidal thoughts, a personal story of abuse. In these cases, offer to go with her as she tells a counsellor or clergy member so that she can get the help she needs. Don't abandon her, but let her know you don't feel qualified to handle these issues.

Interestingly enough, there are two different Hebrew words for gossip. The first is *rakiyl* (don't ask me how to pronounce it!). This word means to travel with confidences — to go around like a travelling salesperson passing on bits of information that were really shared with you alone. Be careful about sharing information about someone if you haven't got her permission. Sometimes what you hear is just so great that you want to share it right away with someone else. Perhaps your friend has just excitedly told you that she is pregnant. She's thrilled; you're thrilled, and you want to tell others so they can be thrilled too. And so you do. The only thing is, your friend wanted to be the one to tell people she is pregnant. So now she is angry and you've got some repair work and apologizing to do! Or perhaps your friend is working her feelings out as she talks to you. Men generally talk for one reason — to convey information. Women talk for all sorts of reasons.

Conveying information is just one of them. We talk to discover our feelings about something; we talk to figure out what it is that we really want to say; and we talk to create intimacy. As your friend is talking to you about her boyfriend, perhaps she is talking to explore her feelings about him. What she doesn't want is you reaching any conclusions and sharing those conclusions with others. As she is venting her frustration about her job, she doesn't want you to share the frustration she is feeling with someone else. She is trusting that you are a safe harbour in which she can share her feelings, frustrations and dreams. Unless she says otherwise ... keep the treasures she has shared with you to yourself!

The other word for gossip is *nirgan*. This word means to roll someone to pieces, and certainly presents a very painful picture. Once I took a fairly new friend, Jane (actually I have changed the names in this instance to protect the innocence of those involved ... I was the one who was an idiot!), to an event where I would be connecting with some long-time friends.

Susan, one of the friends I had known for quite a while, did not really like my new friend Jane. They just didn't click. Actually, looking back, maybe Jane's self-confidence was a threat to Susan. Within a few days, Susan came to me and made some derogatory comments about Jane, and wondered what I was doing with her. Much as it disgusts me to admit this about myself, after Susan made her comments about Jane, I told her not to link me with Jane, that I wasn't that sure about her either (very ugly, isn't it?). Why did I betray Jane? Perhaps because Susan had more power, more to offer, I let her know my allegiance was with her. What I did was 'roll Jane to pieces'. It took me a few months to realize what I had done and why I had done it ... and I was thoroughly disappointed in myself. Nothing is more humbling than realizing the ugliness that can reside inside us! I could've handled the situation in a much better way. When Susan expressed her feelings about Jane, I should have said something like, 'Just give Jane some time. You might really like her after you get to know her'. But because of some insecurity of my own, I betrayed a friend. Now, she never knew. But I did. And I didn't like what my actions said about my character.

Many times we gossip because there is a quality in our friend that really bugs us. And instead of going straight to the woman we are having the problem with, we go to others ostensibly seeking 'their help'. But if any of the others were a true friend they would tell you to go work it out with the person you are having the problem with. Instead of going to others and talking about our friend, we should go to the friend we are actually having the problem with. Rarely is there a need for others to hear about it.

Treasure the friends you have by not gossiping about them. If a problem arises in the friendship — and at some point I am sure it will — go to the woman you are having the issue with. Don't betray the friendship by talking about her with others.

Let's not be the women who love to sit around and gossip about others. Truthfully there is nothing more revolting than being in a room full of women who are busy 'trash-talking' other women. Surely we all have better things to do. We are supposed to be on the same team — making the world a better place to live in.

FRIENDSHIP POWER POINTS

here's what to do . . .

- sshh . . . keep the secret your friend told you to yourself

- if you have a problem with a friend, go straight to her — not to anyone else

- if you have betrayed your friend, be quick to apologize.

CHAPTER SIX

Not forgiving her —

c'mon, we all need a little forgiveness!

We pardon in the degree that we love.

FRANCOIS DE LA ROCHEFOUCAULD

This is the last chapter — I put it last on purpose. Because after reading all the previous chapters, we need to realize that none of our friends are going to do the friendship thing right all the time. I don't do the friendship thing right all the time and I have read countless books on friends, seen movies about friends, made lots of friends and watched the TV show 'Friends' (although I'm not sure just how helpful it is!). There will be times when we all blow it, when we need the forgiveness of our friends.

We need to be willing to forgive when someone makes a mistake, says something they shouldn't (that is usually my mistake), forgets to call you back (okay I've done this too!), is late for the coffee date (oops, guilty again!), doesn't respond the way we think they should and the myriad of other crimes committed against us. Forgiveness doesn't mean pretending the mistake didn't happen, it means acknowledging it and moving on. Use some of the tips from the chapter on fighting fair and work through the issue. Don't just open your heart again to be hurt if you haven't talked about what went wrong. One time my friend abandoned me at a moment when I needed her. Rather than pulling away, which is what I wanted to do, I said to her, 'If you want to be my friend, you can't do this to me again'. I set a boundary with her — she couldn't continue to abandon me and be my friend — while I opened my heart to her again, forgiving her and giving her another chance.

Kathryn truly valued her friendship with Natasha. They both had a zest for life and were equally passionate about their individual pursuits. Natasha was older and more experienced in life, and unfortunately communicated to

Kathryn in ways that sometimes felt degrading. I asked how that made Kathryn feel. She said, 'I felt like at times she would talk down to me, as if I didn't know how to make a decision. I can't help being young or inexperienced. Her daily "little comments" caused me to withdraw and I had to make the decision to forgive her or to abandon the friendship. I realized the friendship was too valuable for me to break it, and so I made the decision to forgive her. And we have a great friendship today.' In order to keep the friendship on the right path, Kathryn needed to forgive Natasha, at the same time letting her know how hurtful the comments had been, and that she didn't want to be talked down to.

Forgiveness means letting go of the offence whether or not the other person says, 'I'm sorry'. Of course, we all need to be willing to say we're sorry. In fact, go ahead and be the first, but don't wait to start forgiving until the other person says they're sorry too. When you wait for an apology before you begin to forgive, you are putting the power to forgive in the other person's hands when it belongs in yours. And, don't wait until you feel like forgiving to forgive, because you never will. I never *feel* like forgiving. I usually feel like yelling and hitting, or withdrawing and giving up on the relationship. However, forgiveness doesn't come out of my feelings, but rather out of my will. I *will* to forgive. I make the choice. Friendship grows on forgiveness, not perfection. Offences are going to come so be ready to forgive. Forgiveness is a way of showing that we accept another's humanity. I believe there are certain relationships I need to maintain and build in order for me to accomplish the mission I have been put on the earth to accomplish. So I can't just give up on a friend when she does something stupid (and none of us are exempt from doing stupid things from time to time).

Forgiveness isn't just a nice thing to do. I believe it is a life-and-death issue. I remember talking with a man who had a life-threatening illness. This very ill man was extremely angry with someone who owed him $300. It didn't appear he was going to get his money back, and he was furious, shaking his fists and going red in the face. When I suggested that he go ahead and forgive the debt and the debtor since it didn't look like he was going to be paid back, he became even more angry. Should the debtor have paid his debts? Absolutely. Did the lender deserve to get his money back? Yes. Was it worth his life? I don't think so. I believe the bitterness inside of him was killing him.

I have known people dying of cancer or struggling with ulcers who refuse to forgive someone who owes them something, or someone who has betrayed them. These people are literally eaten up on the inside by unforgiveness.

Forgiveness can be difficult for us because it pulls against our concept of justice. We want revenge for the offences we've suffered. (Sometimes we won't admit it, but we do!) We want God to bless them with a lighting bolt! You may ask, 'Why should I let them off the hook?' That's the problem: you're hooked. Or we'll say, 'You don't understand how much they hurt me!' But don't you see? They are still hurting you. You are still living the betrayal, the offence, whatever the crime. You don't forgive someone for their sake; you do it for your sake, so that you can be free. Free to love, free to be at peace, free to enjoy the day without being eaten up on the inside.

C'mon girls, let's be quick and willing to forgive each other. Let's not grow up to be little old ladies so full of bitterness that we are a drag to be around. In fact, maybe I have said some things in this book that make you mad ... Well, go ahead and forgive me! Understand that I am doing the best I can with what I know now!

Enjoy your friendships and treat them as the treasures they are!

FRIENDSHIP POWER POINTS

here's what to do . . .

- don't let the bitter seed of unforgiveness grow in your heart

- forgive your friend in the same way you want to be forgiven.

---

[1] Jack Canfield, Mark Victor Hansen, *Chicken Soup for the Soul*, Health Communications, Deerfield Beach, FLA, 1994.

[2] Brenda Hunter, *In the Company of Women*, Multnomah Books, Sisters, Oregon, 1994, p.41.

[3] Cynthia Kersey, *Unstoppable*, Sourcebooks, Inc., Naperville, Illinois, 1988, p.47.

[4] Patricia Skalka, *How to Mend a Friendship*, Reader's Digest, June 1990, p.40.

She
Loves Me
She Loves
Me Not

Sharry

Holly Wagner is known for her challenging, personable and humorous style of addressing life issues such as friendship, marriage and character development. She has previously published *Dumb Things We Do* with HarperCollins*Publishers*. Holly lives in Los Angeles with her husband and two children.

She Loves Me Loves Me She Loves Me Not

Holly Wagner

HarperCollins*Publishers*

HarperCollins*Publishers*

First published in Australia in 2001
by HarperCollins*Publishers* Pty Limited
ABN 36 009 913 517
A member of the HarperCollins*Publishers* (Australia) Pty Limited Group
http://www.harpercollins.com.au

HarperCollins*Publishers*
25 Ryde Road, Pymble, Sydney, NSW 2073, Australia
31 View Road, Glenfield, Auckland 10, New Zealand
77–85 Fulham Palace Road, London, W6 8JB, United Kingdom
Hazelton Lanes, 55 Avenue Road, Suite 2900, Toronto, Ontario M5R 3L2
and 1995 Markham Road, Scarborough, Ontario M1B 5M8, Canada
10 East 53rd Street, New York NY 10022, USA

National Library of Australia Cataloguing-in-Publication data:

Wagner, Holly.
She loves me, she loves me not.
ISBN 0 7322 7010 3.
1. Female friendship. 2. Women – Psychology.
3. Interpersonal relations. I. Title.
158.25082

Cover design: Judi Rowe, HarperCollins Design Studio
Typeset by HarperCollins in 11/14.5 Sabon
Printed and bound in Australia by McPherson's Printing Group
on 79gsm Bulky Paperback White

5 4 3 2 1   01 02 03 04

This little book is dedicated to those women around the planet who, like me, are committed to being better friends ... and thus changing our world one relationship at a time

Author's note

Thank you to my friends ... the sisters of my heart.
    You have helped make my life what it is.
    I am richer and better because of your love and time ...
you are loved forever by me.

Top ten reasons we're such good friends:

10. Neither one of us would ever wear
a 'thong' bikini.

9. Calories we eat together don't count.

8. Shopping, Shopping, Shopping.

7. We have a shared love of telephones.

6. No man is ever going to tell you honestly
if an outfit makes your butt look big.

5. We believe each other's excuses for
missing aerobics.

4. Neither one us ever asks,
'Are you allowed to eat that on your diet?'

3. Chocolate.

2. We can talk mindlessly about our
hair for hours.

and the #1 reason we're such good friends is . . .

1. Every woman's got to have someone to go to
the ladies room with!

Contents

She Loves Me ... Friendship Do's

She Loves Me

Friendship Do's

CHAPTER ONE

Friends are important! —

who else will tell us if we have spinach between our teeth?

True friends are a mirror to the soul,
for they understand the voice of the heart.

FLAVIA

In the not too distant past, I was having some 'challenges' (nice word!) with my husband. He is a wonderful man ... I just couldn't see it on this particular day. My feelings were hurt, and I was frustrated (ever been there?) So what did I do? I called my friend and told her my woes. She listened and made appropriate comments. She let me go on and on.

She is a good enough friend not to let me throw a 'pity party' for too long, or husband bash indefinitely. Eventually she helped me find my own way out of the discouraging place I had found myself in. Thank God for my friend.

. . .

I was in Wales, staring at one of the most magnificent castles I have ever seen (keep in mind, I'm American and to me any castle is amazing!). The view was awe inspiring, almost bringing tears to my eyes. I walked inside and was touched by the history of the place ... wondering who the women were who had lived here in past ages. As I stood just looking and being amazed, the most wonderful thing happened — I grabbed the hand of my friend who was standing next to me and knew that she too was experiencing the same emotions as me. Having someone to share the adventure with made all the difference in the world. Thank God for my friend.

. . .

Tears were streaming down my face as I was confronted with the fact that my son had a physical condition that might require hours of doctor's visits and years of medication (unless we receive that miracle I'm still believing in). Like most parents I hated the thought that my child would have to face any difficulty. As I cried and reached deep inside for strength, I hugged my friend and knew that she was willing to help and be an encouragement along the journey. Thank God for my friend.

. . .

I was bent over double laughing so hard that tears came to my eyes one day as I was shopping (for me one of life's great joys!) in an exclusive area of Sydney, Australia, with my friend. We were trying on very silly outfits in a very sophisticated part of town. No man would have found this moment funny, but we women laughed and laughed until our stomachs ached. Oh the joy of shared laughter! Thank God for my friend.

. . .

Organization is one of life's little challenges for me. I can come up with all sorts of great ideas for a women's seminar, meeting or conference, which will include different speakers, multi-media presentations, props ... but actually carrying through all the steps necessary to accomplish the goal is at times beyond me. My friend often waits patiently while I express my enthusiasm and passion for the event and then quietly asks, 'I suppose you want me to put it all together?' 'Um ... yes ... please ...' I reply. Thank God for my friend.

. . .

There is nothing more exciting for me than to stand on a stage teaching women how to live successful, joyous lives and to look in their faces and know they get what I'm saying. Looking out at the women who are on life's journey with me, determined to finish the course set in front of them, is one of my favourite things. These women make my life rewarding and full. Thank God for my friends.

. . .

And you know the really cool thing? Each one of the above examples is about a different woman. It's great to have so many different women contributing to my life. I treasure them all.

. . .

We each lead very busy lives and sometimes in our busyness, the first thing we give up is the time we spend with our friends. We have jobs, families and activities that all pull at us, and so friends often get put on the back burner. I would like to suggest that the friendships you build are *crucial* to your happiness and your success in this life.

You and I were not created to go through life alone or to solve all of life's problems on our own. We do not have all the answers ourselves. We need each other! There are some of you who have overcome tremendous obstacles on your journey through life, and there are women out there who need to know how you did it. Perhaps you have single handedly raised your children into responsible adults (a miracle for any of us!). I guarantee you there is a woman in your circle of influence who needs to know what you did and how you did it. There are some of you who have overcome tremendous marital obstacles, managed to stay married and still love that man! There are some of us who need to know what you know. Build a relationship with a young woman who could use some of your wisdom. Some of you have lived through tremendous abuse and you have found the path of healing … well, there is a woman out there who is still trapped and needs your help. Maybe you have overcome serious debt and could give someone a few pointers on how to get out of their debt. Your past can help give someone else a future … but only if you are willing to build relationships. There is also someone out there who can help give you hope in what you are going through … but only if you reach out.

I recently read an article in *O, The Oprah Magazine*, that was an interview (actually it was more like eavesdropping on a conversation) between Oprah Winfrey and Jane Fonda. Jane made the observation that she had lived the first two acts of her life and now at sixty-two was beginning act three. She wanted this last act of her life to mean something ... she wanted it to help make sense of the first two acts. She included some of the valuable lessons she has learned in her life, in this interview. I loved reading her comments, because I started thinking, 'THIS IS WHAT IT'S SUPPOSED TO BE LIKE! ... the older woman passing on the lessons of her life to the younger one. I am a woman in my thirties, just at the beginning of act two. I need the older woman to share what she knows and has learned.' Friendships aren't just for you — they are to help those around you. In this interview, Jane Fonda also commented that at the end of her life, she wanted to be surrounded by people whom she loves and who love her. She realized she had some work to do to make that a reality (at least she's starting now).

Friendships are vital. They can be an avenue of hope when it seems like there is no hope. They can be a place of inspiration, they can provide laughter just when you need a smile, and a prayer when you need a miracle. C'mon girls, we need each other. Let's get good at building friendships!

FRIENDSHIP POWER POINTS

here's what to do . . .

- be thankful for the friends you do have
- realize you need your friends . . . their wisdom and their input
  - know that your friends need YOU!

CHAPTER TWO

Accept her —

warts and all!

*****

*If we build on a sure foundation in friendship,
we must love our friends for their sakes
rather than for our own.*

CHARLOTTE BRONTE

'Make a decision ... just make one! And please make it before the end of this century!' It was beginning to be painful to shop with my friend. It took her forever to make up her mind, and she doubted my comment that the blue skirt made her rear end look big. I admit that the blue skirt wasn't really all that bad, I just wanted to get out of

10

this store and on to the next one! And then she had the audacity to tell the store clerk that she would think about it and that we would be back. Not a chance! We were done with this store, there was nothing to think about ... the red or the blue ... how hard was that? Why couldn't she be like me?

. . .

If my friend told me one more time that she needed me to itemize the budget, being careful that the numbers stayed in the correct columns, I was going to scream! And then she proceeded to tell me that there was a computer class that could help me to learn to do budgets using charts and graphs, which she, of course, loved. Fat chance! Why couldn't she be like me?

. . .

Never mind my bloodshot eyes, and the dark circles under them. I was not tired! ... which I proceeded to tell my very bossy friend who was trying to get me to rest. Couldn't she see there was still fun to be had at this leadership training conference and I didn't want to miss it? We got into a very intense discussion (fight) as she attempted to instruct me how to take care of myself: what I should eat, what kind of exercise I needed and how much sleep I should be getting.

What is she ... my mother? Why couldn't she chill out and be more like me?

...

Hippocrates, hundreds of years ago, discovered that there were basically four different personality types. And that all of us are some sort of combination of those four types. When he came up with these four types, it was not to put people in a box, but rather to understand why certain people reacted the way they did. He gave us tools to understand each other better and to learn to communicate with different people much more effectively.

One personality type is the *sanguine*. This is the 'party waiting to happen' — 'confetti in a bottle' person! These people are lively, energetic, and can talk to anyone at any time. Sanguine people are very easy to spot when you walk into a room, because everything about them is open and moving ... their mouth, their hands, and their eyes! They use big gestures to make a point and they laugh frequently and loudly. They make friends easily and love to be with people. These people prevent dull moments, and if you don't know any of them, you should definitely hire some for your next party! They will keep it moving! Because of their energy and zest for life, they are great in front of people — leading meetings or motivating volunteers. When they send you an e-mail it will often include all capitalized words and lots of exclamation marks!!!!!! (Of course, they have to actually remember your address!) On the other hand, sanguine people will often stick their foot in their mouth (because they are talking so much of the time!) and try to dominate conversations. They don't tend to be very organized, and can forget things they are supposed to remember. Generally they are great starters, but finishing projects can be a real challenge! And they can be motivated by feelings rather than reality.

Another personality type is the *melancholy*. These people are the deep thinkers in our society ... they even tend to be genius prone! They can solve problems most of us don't even want to spell! These are the very creative and artistic ones. They actually *use* day planners! (the sanguine type generally buys one because it looks good!). Generally melancholy people are very neat and tidy and like to live in an orderly and organized environment. Not finishing what they start is not even an option — of course the job will be finished! They make friends cautiously, unlike the sanguine who jumps into relationships with both feet, not sure exactly where they will land! Melancholies are faithful and devoted friends, and can be moved to tears with compassion. Most of them have a very dry sense of humour that can keep you laughing at any time. When they send you an e-mail it is grammatically correct with no misspelled words — they actually use the spellchecker! They can, however, also be very negative, finding fault in many situations as if it were buried treasure! They can get perturbed if a house isn't kept just how they think it should be or if someone is late to an appointment with them. They tend to be pessimistic, often seeing the glass half-empty. And because they like perfection and life certainly isn't perfect, they can get depressed when it and other people don't measure up to what they expect or want.

The *choleric* is another personality type. Choleric people are born leaders ... the other personality types learn to be leaders — these are born wanting to take over! They are goal setters and have goals for everything. Unlike the sanguine, these people don't get distracted trying to get from point A to point B. If you don't have an opinion, they will tell you what yours is! And if it takes you too long to finish your sentence, they will finish it for you. In an emergency it is great to have a choleric person around, because they know what to do or will fake it until someone who really does know what to do comes along! Choleric people are energetic and can accomplish many tasks at once, doing whatever it takes. They really like e-mail because the job gets done quicker and you don't have to chit-chat about a lot of 'trivial stuff'. Cholerics are not easily discouraged and move quickly to action. Like the sanguine, they are great in front of people because of their confidence. They can, however, try to drive people rather than lead them. And they can leave out the fun in their quest to get the job done. They also can step over people and their feelings on their journey to get the job done ... ouch!

The *phlegmatic* is the other personality type. Phlegmatic people can be difficult to spot, because they are a little like chameleons — becoming whatever is necessary in any given situation. They are not extremely anything. Generally they are easy going and relaxed, peaceful and agreeable. These people can be very easy to get along with because they are great listeners and compassionate towards others and their problems. They can, however, be unenthusiastic and indecisive. It takes them quite a while to make up their mind about most things, but generally they prefer the status quo. It might take a stick of dynamite to get them to move or to try something new! They prefer to wear the most casual thing a situation would allow them to. I once heard Florence Littauer teaching and she said that phlegmatics can be a bit lazy ... if standing becomes too tiring, they will lean; if leaning becomes exhausting, they will sit ... until eventually they are practically lying down!

I love learning and studying about the different personality types trying to figure out which one I am (actually that is not so difficult to work out ... I am the loud party-waiting-to-happen sanguine!), but the higher purpose is so that we can better understand someone else. The goal is to understand them and value them, not make them wrong. There is no wrong personality.

Realize that someone with a different personality to you will handle situations differently to you. This does not make them wrong. Understanding and applying this concept has not only helped me accept my different friends, it has actually helped around our office. While each personality type can do many kinds of jobs, generally there is a job where we each will thrive. We generally found that someone with the melancholy personality is better suited to a job that requires extreme attention to detail. Usually a phlegmatic is best if we need someone to counsel people through grief. If the job requires constant interaction with people, like customer service, a sanguine will thrive. A choleric is great for those jobs requiring someone with drive and initiative. For an office to be fully effective, people of all personality types are needed. For my life to be richer, for me to fulfil my destiny, I need to be building relationships with people who have different personalities.

So instead of thinking: 'That girl is just too picky and detailed for me!', learn to value her for her organizational skills.

Instead of thinking: 'That girl is too hyper and too scattered!', make the choice to value her for her energy and spontaneity.

Instead of thinking: 'That girl is too pushy, and always in a hurry to tell me what to do,' be grateful that she's in your life, because you probably go more places and see more things because of her.

Instead of thinking: 'That girl is a slug and hardly says two words!', be grateful for her peaceful presence in a chaotic world.

We often look only for people who are just like us to be our friends. How many great friendships are we missing out on if we do this?

FRIENDSHIP POWER POINTS

here's what to do . . .

- talk with your friend about the many ways your personalities are different

- apologize to your friend for the times you may have been impatient or critical

- be glad she is how she is!

CHAPTER THREE

Open your circle of friends —

got room for one more?

＊＊＊＊＊

*No one person can possibly combine all the
elements supposed to make up what everyone
means by friendship.*

FRANCIS MARION CRAWFORD

As a friend, I try not only to value the friendship, but
also to value the person. There is nothing more
wonderful than spending time with someone who truly
values you ... someone you *know* likes you. I want my
friends to feel valued, and one of the ways I can ensure this
is to love who they are — not who I wish they were. Love

19

the differences between you and your friends — don't just tolerate them, but love them! It is not always easy because sometimes the differences between us seem insurmountable!

Build an ever-increasing circle of friendships, keeping our hearts and minds open to accepting friends who are different from us.

Plenty of people let differences between them get in the way of friendship. Let's not be like that!

Find value in making friends with someone from a different generation. We can learn so much from those younger and older than us. My marriage survived a very rocky patch because I took the time to develop a relationship with an older woman who could help me through it. (She wouldn't let me kill him ... which of course I was considering! ... and she reminded me of some of the reasons I loved him — I had conveniently forgotten these!) My first child also survived babyhood because I spent time with experienced mothers. I enjoyed spending time with other first-time mothers, but I truly got help from women just a little older than me. Find a woman who has climbed the mountain you want to scale and let her open your eyes to new possibilities. Also find a younger woman — someone who is perhaps struggling with a giant you have already killed. She needs you, and there are things you can learn from her ... maybe some new, fun way to dress or wear your hair! My friend Anjanette is fourteen years younger than I am. She keeps me in touch with new thoughts, styles and ideas. And because I believe one of my most important jobs on the planet is to encourage, inspire, train and teach the generation of girls right behind me, she keeps me on my toes. I can't just tell her the best way to live her life — I have to model it. No pressure there! We have both been invaluable to each other.

Make friends with someone from a different culture. The world is a big place, but we can make it smaller if, within our own communities, we are pulling down racial barriers. We can make a difference in our own lives and in the world if we go beyond our comfort zone and truly build relationships with people who look and think differently to us. Recently I was asked to be a guest on a daytime talk show in the USA. Initially they wanted me to discuss how women of different cultures could be friends. I was very happy to do this, because not only do I think it is possible for women of different cultures to be friends, I think it is crucial. I have started small groups within our church bringing together women of very different backgrounds and we managed to move from being acquaintances to being true friends … so I know it is possible and I wanted to share my experience. A few days before I was to tape the show, they called me and said there were going to be a few changes. Instead of a show demonstrating that women of different cultures could be friends, they wanted me to come on and basically fight with someone who was different to demonstrate why we couldn't be friends. Needless to say I declined to go on the show. I realize the organizers were after high ratings — a fight does generate them. I was just not willing to be a part of this. I believe one of the reasons I have been put on the planet is to demonstrate what healthy relationships are like and teach others how to have them. I truly think the world is ready for some help and that people are not just looking for silly entertainment on TV.

Build a friendship with someone who has different interests from you. Of course it is important to share interests, and naturally we are drawn to those with whom we share dreams and goals. That's great! I'm just suggesting that we open our circle to include someone who likes different things. Maybe you have never been a sports enthusiast (you are still grumbling over the fact that you were always picked last for the softball team!). Sport never has to be your favourite thing, but your life will be richer if you spend time with your friend who loves sport. Even if you never end up being Ms Jock, at least your friend will feel important because you took the time to do something with her that didn't come easily to you. Maybe you like Country and Western music (don't be shocked ... there are a few of us!) and your friend is into jazz ... how about going with her to a jazz concert? Perhaps your music tastes will expand, but if not, you will have made her feel important because you supported her in something. What if you hate coffee? So? Go with her to that café anyway! Spending some time together is priceless.

C'mon girls ... instead of trying to mould our friends in our own image, let's love them just how they are! Let's accept certain limits. We can't be angry with someone who is tall wanting them to be shorter, but sometimes we communicate that about hidden things. While we should all be growing and becoming stronger in certain areas of our lives, certain things in people are not going to change. Let's accept people for who they are. The truth is, they will only ever be a better version of themselves and not a whole different person! As the American writer Allan Gurganus said, 'If you are a person's friend, you don't harp on things you know are past their ever changing'.

Look to build friendships with those of different personalities, age groups and backgrounds. Will it be easy? No! It is never easy getting out of our comfort zone! But I do know our lives will be the richer for it!

FRIENDSHIP POWER POINTS

here's what to do . . .

- love the differences between you and your friend
- don't try to change her — love her the way she is
- spend time with a woman from a different generation . . . younger and older
- spend time with a woman who has different interests from yours.

24

CHAPTER FOUR

Be loyal through the ups and downs —

and I'm not talking about our weight!

*****

*Trouble is a sieve through which we sift
our acquaintances. Those too big
to pass through are our friends.*

ARLENE FRANCIS

Being loyal, according to Mr Webster, means being devoted to, to stand by, to fulfil promises. It also means to forsake any ambition that compromises the relationship. What I have found is that most people are loyal as long as it's convenient. But when something better or when someone who can do more for us comes along, we ditch the old for the new.

As children, we're friends with the kid who has the best toys or the best back yard (or, in my case, the cutest brother!). If some kid comes along who has more — a car, a better stereo, a more handsome brother — whatever — we start hanging out with them.

When you're loyal, you're committed through the difficult times. I used to think that every relationship involved a 50–50 commitment. But that is so wrong! In every relationship, there are times when one person is doing most of the giving. Sometimes it's 70–30, sometimes it's 40–60, and sometimes one person is so weak or in such a tough spot that it is 100–0! It can be exhausting listening to a friend who is going through a tough, emotional time (not for you phlegmatics of course!). But as a loyal friend we are supportive as our friend works through her pain. After all, there will come a time when we will need the same support! If we are loyal we stick by our friends in the hard times.

> One could not but be moved by the story of the soldier who asked his officer if he might go out into the 'No Man's Land' between the trenches in World War I to bring in one of his comrades who lay grievously wounded. 'You can go,' said the officer, 'but it's not worth it. Your friend has probably been

killed, and you will throw your own life away.' But the man went. Somehow he managed to get to his friend, hoist him onto his shoulder, and bring him back to the trenches. The two of them tumbled in together and lay at the bottom of the trench. The officer looked very tenderly on the would-be-rescuer, and then he said, 'I told you it wouldn't be worth it. Your friend is dead and you are mortally wounded.' 'It was worth it, though, sir,' he said. 'How do you mean, "worth it"? I tell you your friend is dead.' 'Yes sir,' the boy answered, 'but it was worth it, because when I got to him he was still alive, and he said to me, "Jim, I knew you'd come".'[2]

There was a time when I was so frustrated in my marriage that I was ready to throw in the towel (or throw it at him!). During this time, I was very self-focused and I know I was not very giving to my friends. However, I did have one friend, Diane, who stood by my side. She gave me some great bits of advice, but more than that, I felt loved by her. She met me for coffee, lunch, a good cry ... whatever. She let me pour my heart out to her time and time again. At this time in our friendship, I was giving about 0% to her and she was doing all of the giving. I can see now how it could have been very frustrating to her! But she stood by me in my tough time, and her loyalty to me and to my marriage did pull me to safety.

I have noticed, however, that often it is harder for someone to be loyal when things are going really well in their friend's life. Recently, I was in a room full of women. (Some men came in, took one look, and quickly backed out! … too much estrogen I guess!) One of my friends was there and asked me what was going on with me, and when I filled her in on the latest in my life (some up-coming television stuff in an arena that was new for all of us) she was thrilled. She got so excited for me. There was another woman there who didn't really want to hear what was going on. She asked no questions and just turned away. Perhaps she just wasn't interested, and that's okay (we all have our own lives we're living), but, as my friend, I wish she had shown *some* interest in my life even though it might have been difficult for her. A lot of the wonderful things going on in my life are the result of finding what God put me on the earth to accomplish and just living it out. I am not more special than anyone else … and I know that.

It's fairly easy to rejoice with a friend when something good happens to her and you aren't particularly interested in it happening to you. A few years ago, after four and a half years of training, I was ready to take my black belt test in karate. I invited some friends to come watch the test and quietly cheer me on as I sweated my way to a black belt. Now, of course, it was easy for them to get excited about this particular achievement of mine, because none of them wanted anything to do with high kicks, punching bags or being knocked on their rear end! So they could freely get excited for me. Maybe you know someone who is having her tenth child (AAAGH!) ... it is easy to rejoice with her, because you don't want anything to do with ten children! But what if something happens to your friend that you wish would happen to you? Can you rejoice with her then?

What if you're single and your friend who has been single (but for not nearly as long as you have!) is getting married. Can you be happy, truly happy for her? Or are you feeling things like:

> 'Hey *I'm* the one who went to Jenny Craig and lost all of this weight!'
> 'What's the deal, *I'm* the one who had my eyeliner and lips tattooed for around-the-clock beauty!'

'*I'm* the one who's spent hours learning about football!'

'*I* even took classes on relinquishing the remote control!'

'What's the deal with this? It should be me getting married first! *I'm* the one who's been a bridesmaid seventeen times!'

Why is it that we sometimes can't rejoice with someone in the good times? Perhaps it is because of jealousy or envy … and those are not emotions to be proud of! If you do find yourself feeling jealous, it should indicate to you a slight sense of insecurity and perhaps frustration because you aren't aware of your purpose and destiny. That can be worked on! Someone else accomplishing her goals should just encourage you that it can be done. Someone else fulfilling her purpose doesn't take away from you fulfilling yours. We were each put on the planet to accomplish our own unique destiny. My destiny is linked to other people's destinies. I believe that when our friends are walking on their paths it should thrill us, because I truly believe that as our friends fulfil their destiny, we will too.

Can you rejoice with your friend, even during those times when it might be tough to do so? Can you be happy for your friend as she discovers she is pregnant with her third child and you have been trying to conceive for ten years? The desire for a child as well as the desire for a meaningful relationship are God-given ones, so I can understand how it would be a challenge to be happy for your friend, or even be around her as she celebrates such a momentous occasion. And on the flip side, if you are the one pregnant or getting married, can you be sensitive and patient while your friend works it out? Danielle Schlass in *Working Mother* magazine gives advice to a pregnant woman with a friend who has been trying to conceive.

> 'While your pregnancy is good news to you, it may have been devastating to your friend. You won't be able to hide your burgeoning belly or the new addition to the family from your friend, but a lasting friendship is possible if you broach the subject in a very sensitive manner', says Linda Applegarth, EdD, director of psychological services at the Center for Reproductive Medicine and Infertility at Cornell University Medical Center in New York City. Applegarth suggests that if you have accidentally blurted out your impending joy to your neighbour (which is understandable), try apologizing for the insensitive way it may have come

across. Explain to her that you understand that this is a difficult situation for her, but you value the friendship and you'll be there for her if she needs you. Let any discussion about the baby be on your friend's terms. Let her know that while you're happy to answer any questions about your pregnancy, if she doesn't want to talk about it, that's fine too. Let her be the one to bring it up.[3]

If we would only be willing for a moment to see life from our friend's perspective, then we could be sensitive when necessary and be able to rejoice when it is important for our friend that we do. Taking the focus off ourselves is an important step in displaying loyalty.

In Los Angeles, where I live, quite a few of my friends are involved in the entertainment industry. There are times when more than one of them will be auditioning for the same part. My challenge to them is to be happy for their friend, and not withdraw with jealousy if she gets the part. I'm not saying this comes easy for most of us, I just know that to be loyal to a friend, we must stick by them in both the good and bad times.

FRIENDSHIP POWER POINTS

here's what to do . . .

- stand by your friend when she is going through a hard time

- support your friend when something great happens to her . . . don't be jealous!

friendship do's

CHAPTER FIVE

Friendships take time —

think crockpot ... not microwave!

*The growth of true friendship may be
a lifelong affair.*

SARAH ORNE JEWETT

We are a part of the instant generation ... the drive-through crowd. Generally if something takes longer than ten minutes we won't wait. We are the 'I want it and I want it now' people! I am the same way. I don't like waiting for anything. But friendship is different ... it grows over time. And not just with the passing of time itself, but with the time we invest in the friendship.

Understanding the way friendship works is a little like looking at a puzzle. There are many pieces in a puzzle and each is a different size or shape. And there are many different people in our life, each a different size piece in our heart's friendship 'puzzle'. Generally most people start out as acquaintances. And our puzzle is filled with these pieces. These are the people we know a little about — the waitress at our favourite café, the student in our chemistry class, the other soccer mum, the girl who works downstairs or our hairdresser. Other pieces in our puzzle, which are a little bigger, are the people we work with or see on a regular basis. We could belong to the same sports team, book club or church. We are not really intimate with these people but we might know a lot about them. Their pieces in our puzzle are bigger than the acquaintance pieces. The next biggest pieces in our puzzle are friends ... those with whom we are working out the issues of friendship that I am writing about in this book. Then come the largest and probably the fewest pieces in the puzzle — our intimate friendships ... the sisters of our heart. Not everyone will become an intimate friend and that's okay, although I think it is definitely important to have more than one intimate friend! In fact, I'm currently teaching my daughter that it's good to have more than one best friend. One person can't and shouldn't be everything to you. That's way too much pressure to put on someone! (Your husband should be one of your intimate friends ... although not the only one or you will drive him nuts!)

How does someone go from being an acquaintance to being an intimate friend? The first step I believe has to be some form of agreement. This doesn't mean you agree about everything, but there are some basic core values that you agree on. You've heard the expression 'birds of a feather flock together' — the reason they flock together is because they are heading in the same direction. Your intimate friends will also be heading the same way as you. Perhaps your friendship begins with an agreement about commitment to family or your faith, or perhaps you and your friends are very committed to careers or to a common global cause.

What is it that is deeply important to you? It will also be important to those people who are your intimate friends. These agreements may start out as unstated, but the more you spend time with someone, the more their values become evident. Eventually you will talk about them, discovering if you truly agree with your friend. Obviously, we respect the different characteristics of our friends like taste and style — learning to find the joy and humour in them, but our intimate friends have the same or very similar core values. They may not be expressed the same way, but at the heart of the issue, they are similar. For example, if honouring and preserving your marriage is a core value of yours, then though you might have a friend who regularly cheats on her husband, she shouldn't or wouldn't be an intimate friend.

Not only should there be some form of agreement in the core values between friends, but in order for a piece in our friendship puzzle to grow from acquaintance to friend or intimate friend, there must be an investment of time. Taking time out of an already busy schedule (I'm sure you've got one of those too!) to spend with a friend is not always an easy thing to manage, but I have learned that my life is much richer if I do. Recently I was teaching a seminar about friendships. After teaching a few of the principles that I have mentioned in this book, a woman came up to me and said, 'I know friendships are important, I just couldn't manage to fit them into my very busy life. Thanks for giving me some ideas about how to make my friendships stronger. I will now take the time.' She was just one of several women there who realized how important friendships are in their already overloaded lives. Women just like you. Women with busy lives … jobs … careers … husbands … children. C'mon, give your friends a piece of your time.

Quite a few of my intimate friends live in other states, even in other countries. But I don't let that be an excuse … some people are supposed to be forever friends, so I do whatever it takes to maintain the friendship. I have spent a number of hours with my friends Chris and Dianne at airport lounges as they layover at Los Angeles airport. Getting to the airport is always a nightmare … but the joy of connecting with my friends is worth it. I have taken short flights to another city to catch my friend Shanelle as she jets around the globe. I have a husband, two children, and a job that requires my time and my heart, so I don't get many of these trips, but I take them whenever I can. No, it is never convenient. Friendship rarely is. If I am given the choice between a new couch and a trip to see my friend Bobbie, I'll take the trip every time. My relationships with my friends are eternal — the couch will need re-upholstering in a few years!

It should be much easier to find the time to build the relationships with the women in your own city or neighbourhood. If you have small children, meet at the park or some brave woman's home! If the children are older and at school, meet with your friends for coffee every now and then. If you are working, take an evening once in a while to be with the girls. It can be done. To build the relationship from acquaintance to friend, you need to invest time, and there are lots of creative ways to do that. My friend Lisa gets together with some women every second month in a book club. Cokie Roberts, co-anchor of ABC News' *This Week with Sam Donaldson and Cokie Roberts,* says that her daughter is also in a book club where the women find it a great excuse to get together and have a glass of wine and talk. In a *Woman's Day* article, Cokie comments that a book club is a nice way for women to get together because you have a different book to discuss each time you meet and the conversations more than likely branch off into everything else that's going on in their lives. In generations gone by, women of different ages connected around creating a quilt, raising a barn, birthing a baby or just over a cup of coffee in someone's home. But now, with so many women in the work force, we must get creative and not give up on making the connection with our friends. Often a friendship falls through the cracks just because we haven't given it any time. Go ahead ... water that friendship and see if it grows!

There are also some simple ways to give your friends some time. I love cards. I love shopping for cards. I love buying cards to give to my friends. I love receiving cards. Whenever I get on a plane, I take the first few moments to jot down a thought and put it on a card to mail to a friend. How hard is that? When I receive a note or card from my friend it touches my heart deeply, not just because of what the card says, but because it shows that for a few moments in her day, my friend was thinking of me. I would imagine the same would apply for her, so I take the time to let her know how important she is to me. A phone call, fax or e-mail can also be a quick way to connect with a friend and build the friendship that will last. It really isn't that hard. Sometimes I call my friend Bobbie and I really have nothing earth shattering to say (she lives in Sydney, Australia, I'm in Los Angeles ... at the prices of the phone calls I should be saying something earth shattering!). It's just a way to stay connected. Sometimes we'll start to say good-bye and one of us will think of about five more things to say! And often I'll call a friend, reach an answering machine (doesn't anybody stay at home anymore?), and leave a quick 'hello,

I was thinking of you' message. I love e-mail (especially when I can't find any postage stamps!). It doesn't have to be a long message, just a quick sentence will do. Any of the above will work — just take the time to connect with your friend. I promise you it will touch her heart.

For a relationship to grow into an intimate friendship, it also takes both of you wanting it to. If you see the possibility of a friendship growing, invest in it. If your want-to-be-friend sees and invests too, you have struck gold! Don't, however, spend too much time wanting to be friends with someone who doesn't want to be friends with you (there are plenty of women in the world who do want to be your friend!). Realize that for this time in history, she may just be an acquaintance or casual friend and that's okay. (Here's a tip for free ... this concept applies to our relationships with men too. When the man you are dating doesn't want a relationship any more, let it end graciously. Show respect for yourself and him; don't force, manipulate or pressure.) It is a drag to feel pressured into being someone's friend; so don't do that. There are other women waiting to be your friend! Many times as children we are possessive about our friends ... not really wanting them to have other friends. We feel abandoned and hurt if they develop a new friendship. We can't be like this. Really! We should rejoice! You want your friend to have lots of friends contributing to her life. You cannot be everything to her … it would wear you out. And your friend can't be everything to you. We each have strengths, and the different people you allow into your heart will bring different strengths into your life. I can't say this enough — keep your heart open.

A tragic event occurred at Harvard University in 1995. At the end of the spring semester, Sinedu Tadesse, a third-year undergraduate student from Addis Ababa, took a hunting knife and stabbed her roommate Trang Phuong Ho over and over again. Thao Nguyen, a guest who had spent the night, and who was a best friend of Trang's, was also stabbed. After Sinedu murdered the friend, who in her mind had abandoned her, Sinedu hanged herself. Sinedu had felt that, in Trang, she had found her one true friend, and so felt abandoned when she heard that Trang would no longer be rooming with her the following year. Instead of welcoming Trang's friend Thao into their circle, she became jealous and possessive with disastrous results. Now, this is certainly an extreme situation, and most of us would never murder someone, but perhaps what we do is pull away when our friend makes another friend. Let's not.

Surely our heart is big enough for one more person. I love the phrase that I used to sing at summer camps, 'Make new friends, but keep the old; one is silver and the other is gold.' Those of you with daughters, encourage them to follow this principle ... it will help them immensely as they grow. And the best way for them to get it is for them to see you model an open, easy, accepting friendship. Possessiveness, a desire for exclusivity, and a view of other people as a threat to the friendship are all signs of inappropriate dependence.

The pieces in our friendship 'puzzle' will change shapes. Some will grow smaller and some will become bigger. We need to let people come and go. Always keep your heart open for friends. You could meet one of the best friends you will ever have next week! The borders of our puzzle should always be expanding, meaning your life should continue to enlarge with people. I'm sure, because you are human like me, you have been hurt and betrayed a time or two by friends. Yes, it is very painful. But please don't allow the hurt to become bitterness which causes you to close your heart to people! Friends, who *all* start out just as people we meet, are truly one of heaven's greatest gifts to us. Let's embrace this gift!

FRIENDSHIP POWER POINTS

here's what to do . . .
- put time into your friendship
- write a note, make a call, send an e-mail . . . SOMETHING!
- don't be exclusive . . . keep your heart open for more and more friends.

CHAPTER SIX

Share secrets —

yep, you need to tell her ...

*Oh, the comfort, the inexpressible comfort of feeling
safe with a person, having neither to weigh thoughts
nor measure words, but pouring them all right out,
just as they are, chaff and grain together; certain that
a faithful hand will take and sift them, keep what is
worth keeping, and then with the breath of kindness
throw the rest away.*

DINAH MARIA MULOCK CRAIK

These times are going to take real friends. Jack Nicholson
said in the movie *A Few Good Men*, 'You can't handle

the truth!'. (Actually, I went to see the movie for the Tom Cruise factor ... the Nicholson statement was a bonus!) We need friends today who can handle the truth. According to a USA TODAY Snapshot®, forty-three percent of the women polled said they would rather share a worry or fear with a friend than with their spouse, a relative or physician. So, the truth is that we would *like* to share the secrets of our heart, our dreams and fears with a friend, but for one reason or another, we aren't always willing.

I remember an instance in our church that involved a young couple. They had been coming to the church for a while, always remaining on the outskirts of the congregation. One day they came to me as their pastor and described a crisis they were in. I felt badly for them and certainly offered what help I could. But what made me sad was that they had no one with whom they had been intimate, no real friend that could stand by them and help them through this situation. Life can be tough. (You've probably figured that out by now!) We need friends who truly *know* us, so that the tough times we face are bearable. I read a comment by an actress who admitted that her inability to truly be intimate has been at the core of her marriage break-ups. And she knows this is what keeps her friends, even her daughter, at a distance. At least now she is realizing that in order for her life to finish strong, she must develop the ability to be intimate. So must you and I. Yes, it might be scary ... but a life without intimacy is really no life at all.

Terri Apter and Ruthellen Josselson in their book *Best Friends* agree that:

> things happen to us, and we do things we need to talk about ... and yet we don't want everyone to know. We share our feeling of danger and insecurity, or we confess to behaviour that we feel is bad or humiliating. We can tell a friend because she'll be on our side. We count on her to see things from our point of view, to support us, even if she may disagree with what we've done.[4]

If our friend doesn't see things from our point of view, or fails to support us, then we must deal with the feelings of betrayal that will follow. I'll talk about this soon.

Most of us have a dream in our heart. We need a friend we can share that dream with, so that when it seems like our dream is not coming to pass, they can continue to encourage us. Without the encouragement of my friends, there are many things I would have given up on. But my friends couldn't have encouraged me if I hadn't first opened my heart and shared its secrets ... dreams as well as fears. Sometimes we try so hard to be independent. We really weren't created to live independently. We are meant to live *inter*dependently — linked to each other. This happens when we are willing to be intimate. I heard a saying once: 'a friend is someone who knows the song in your heart and can sing it back to you when you have forgotten the words'. They can only sing it back if you have shown them your heart (and actually, with my voice, it would be better for the song to be in my heart and for someone else to sing it!).

To build a friendship and to keep one from dying requires intimacy. Let's get real! We need to get over our fear of betrayal so that we can open our hearts. One thing that keeps us from opening our hearts to someone is our fear of being hurt or let down. If you are alive, on the planet and in your body, you have probably been betrayed. I haven't met anyone who hasn't been. To keep betrayal to a minimum, however, there are some guidelines to being intimate. We can't just share our deepest fear, secret or even dream with someone who hasn't proven that they can handle it. Don't share the story of your life with someone you have just met! When we share something with someone without really knowing how she'll handle it, we risk betrayal, which is certainly painful. When we wait until we feel we know and trust someone, we still might be betrayed, but at least we have been wiser with whom we share our secrets. We trust someone, based not on her potential, but on the results in her life. I've heard people say, 'Well, they didn't mean to do all of that hurtful stuff to you; they have a good heart'. No, if someone has a good heart, then they don't consistently hurt you. We can't get sentimental and continue to open our heart to that girl we've 'known since kindergarten' if she continues to betray us. If she gossips about others, she will gossip about you. To test whether someone can handle intimacy, share something small with her. If she keeps that to herself, then you can share something bigger. Let someone prove herself faithful with a small portion of your heart before they are given a bigger portion. (It's just like at work. We wouldn't promote anyone to a better position if they hadn't been successful at the first one.) Susan L. Taylor wrote in her book, *In the Spirit*, 'Not everyone is healthy enough to have a front-row seat in our lives'. The more we look for respect, the more our own character grows. The more we look for love and truth in the world around us, the easier it will become to decide who gets to sit in the front row of our life. The bottom line is: yes, we need to be intimate with friends, but there are some guidelines to follow about who we are intimate with.

There are some simple gestures that create an atmosphere of intimacy between people, such as eating together, working on a project together, the giving of gifts and words (either written or spoken). Have a meal with your friend every now and then (especially those meals where you don't count calories!). An atmosphere of intimacy can develop when we laugh and talk over a meal. Many of my relationships have grown as my friends and I have worked together on a project ... whether it is a women's meeting, something at my children's school or some kind of home-decorating thing (which I am pathetic at, by the way!). The time spent together, the late nights, the endless cups of coffee all provide an atmosphere of intimacy. There are ways to provide opportunities for intimacy, but true intimacy involves communication. Sooner or later we have to talk, really share with our friend, if we want the friendship to be meaningful. Terri Apter and Ruthellen

Josselson say it like this: 'Talk is the currency of friendship. The route to sympathy, understanding and connection is through talk'. If this sounds uncomfortable to you, then begin with asking questions of your friend, such as:

> What is the most exciting thing that has happened to you so far?
> What is your biggest fear?
> What is the dumbest thing you have ever done?
> What do you think you are really good at?
> What is your most embarrassing moment? (this should provide a lot of laughs!)
> What do you love most about your husband (or boyfriend)?
> What is something you want to accomplish before you die?

These are just ideas. But asking questions conveys to your friend you are interested and as she answers, she opens her heart to you — a true treasure.

While intimacy is crucial for any friendship to truly develop, timing is also essential. Be conscious of the kind of day your friend has had, the season she is in. If you just got an amazing promotion and you call your friend only to find out she was fired, waiting a day or two before you share your news might be best. You want to give her a chance to rejoice with you, and she very well might — just give her a day to recover. What you can do is listen to her. A verse in the New Testament tells us to 'rejoice with those who rejoice and weep with those who weep'. I also learned this lesson with my husband. If I have some great news (maybe I'm pregnant or won the lottery or something!), then I wait until he is in a place where he can rejoice with me (but not when he is in a meeting!).

I also think it is important to tell your friend how much you value the friendship ... that you don't take it for granted. Don't wait until your friend's funeral to say the nice things you think about her. Tell her now! Not too long ago I was at a funeral and heard friends and family alike saying some really wonderful things about the person who was lying in the casket. I remember wishing that the deceased person could hear the terrific things being said about them, because I was pretty sure no one had told them those things while they were alive. How sad!

Recently I received a letter from a friend, close in heart, but who in reality lives thousands of miles away. She wrote words I will always treasure.

Dear Holly

It was great to talk with you on the phone. Oh, how I miss the uniqueness of our friendship ... being able to share ideas, exchange dreams, be grumpy, sad, silly, a slave to funky fashion ... with you I can share times when I am feeling lost ... you have held my hand through life ... what a gift ... I am grateful ...

Sigh ... how wonderful to have a friend who shares her feelings.

A few months ago, I was visiting my friend and saw a letter that I had written to her tacked to the wall in her kitchen. It was just a silly little note in which I expressed gratitude for our friendship. As I was looking at the note and smiling, she told me that a few teenage girls, who were friends of her sons, had been in the house and also looked at the note. Their response was interesting. They had looked at her longingly and said they hoped one day they would have a friend who would write them a note like that. We all crave deep friendships. We were born with a need for them. But they don't come just by wanting them. They come as we give the time, share the dreams of our heart, and are willing to be intimate. I feel as a woman in my thirties, one of my jobs is to model healthy friendships for those in the generation after mine ... and I take that job very seriously.

In fact, I am now training my daughter about this. (Another tip for free for you mothers out there. Your daughter learns how to connect and be intimate with her friends as she watches you ... so what are you modelling? ... just a question.) When my daughter Paris was seven, she told me how much she liked her friend Audrey. I asked her if she had told Audrey. She told me she hadn't and looked at me strangely for asking. I suggested that next time she talked to Audrey she tell her that she's glad they're friends. It wasn't long before they were on the phone, and I heard my daughter tell Audrey how glad she was for their friendship. Tell your friend how much you count on her friendship. Tell her the things you love about her. Tell her the dreams in your heart. Tell her what you are afraid of — just tell her.

FRIENDSHIP POWER POINTS

here's what to do . . .

- share a dream and a fear with your friend

- once your friend has proven faithful with a small piece of your heart . . . share a bigger piece with her

- ask your friend a question from page 51

- let your friend know that she is a treasure.

CHAPTER SEVEN

Laugh a lot —

it's fun *and* it burns calories!

The total absence of humour renders life impossible.
COLETTE (SIDONIE GABRIELLE)

Life can be serious enough. It is crucial that we take the time to have fun ... to laugh! Most of us do very important, rather serious things for a lot of our day — our jobs, our children, our husbands or boyfriends, our sick mother-in-law, keeping the house clean, figuring out what we are going to have for dinner, cleaning up doggy poop ... you know ... quite a bit of serious stuff! It is important to let go every now and then.

I do love to laugh — the real laughter that makes you hold your stomach (I've heard that real laughter is as good as sit-ups … and much more fun, don't you think?) makes you wipe your eyes clean of the mascara that is running down your cheeks. The best laughter is shared laughter. An intimacy is wrought when you laugh with a friend. There have been studies done about the healing aspects of laughter — laughter and a positive attitude help bolster your immune system, whereas anger and stress can destroy it. Norman Cousins, after he was diagnosed with a degenerative spinal disease, rented comedy movies that made him laugh and then allowed him to get a couple hours of painless sleep. And in 1992, researchers at Duke University found a fifty percent five-year mortality rate among unmarried heart patients without a close friend or confidant, compared with only a seventeen percent mortality rate for heart patients with a spouse, confidant or both. Laughter is definitely healing, and shared laughter is even better. There is a proverb that says, 'A cheerful heart makes medicine even better'. Laughter releases some kind of endorphin that promotes healing. So, not only does laughing feel good, create abs of steel, and promote intimacy in a friendship, it can also help bring about healing!

In this book I have talked about some very real, somewhat serious, ways to make our friendships better, but it is important to remember to also have fun. We need to do things together with our friends that help create light heartedness. We need to just do some fun things. Some people are SO serious — it really is a drag to be around them. You probably have at least one quirky friend who makes you smile. Spend time with her ... not trying to make her serious, but enjoying her ability to be carefree. Go to a silly movie together and laugh out loud. Go to a card store and read each other the funny cards. I love to do this ... and invariably I end up passing the card to a stranger so she can enjoy the joke too!

Do relaxing things together. Go get a manicure ... or a massage ... or a tan ... or a coffee. Go for a run ... or a walk. Watch the sunrise ... or the sunset. Try a new restaurant on your girls' night out. *Have* the occasional girls' night out! Have a slumber party ... you are never too old for slumber parties! Go shopping and try on the craziest clothes. I was in Dallas one time with my friends Kelly and Laura. We went into a store in a fairly conservative neighbourhood, and began putting on the wildest clothes combinations. We even photographed the fun. Days later we were still laughing at how silly we looked. And it cost nothing.

Create and enjoy the fun in friendships!

FRIENDSHIP POWER POINTS

here's what to do . . .

- don't take yourself so seriously
- do silly things and relaxing 'girl things' with your friends.

---

[1] Shoebox Greetings, a division of Hallmark, Hallmark Cards USA.

[2] James S. Hewitt, *Illustrations Unlimited*, Tyndale House Publishers, Wheaton, Illinois, 1988, p.226.

[3] Danielle Schlass, *Working Mother*, November 2000, p.48.

[4] Terri Apter, Ruthellen Josselson, *Best Friends*, Three Rivers Press, NY, 1999, p. 147.